DEFEATING THE OPIATE DEMON

David Galindo Rivera

DISCLAIMER:

Just because this worked for me, does not mean it
will work for you. Discipline and desire are required. If
you want to change, you will! Defeating the opiate demon was
a matter of life and death. Please consult your physician before
trying any of this.

ACKNOWLEDGMENTS

First and foremost, I humbly thank Jesus(God) for saving my life. I will never doubt nor deny you. I love our peace of marriage. Special thanks to Peter Egoscue, and Dr. Ben Benjamin for educating about self-care.

Tony Ward and Dr. Ron Burnett are amazing healers.

Adam Ibarra and Belinda Olivas take great pictures. Don Miguel Ruiz' book, changed my way of thinking. Terry inspired me to find Turmeric. Lamar Mathurin was nice enough to create my cover page.

We all need to love one another. This will hopefully reach and help many.

SUMMARY OF PROCESS

My opiate demon started because of a back injury. I fell injuring my back. Falls are the most frightening and sudden instances. You can hardly brace yourself. Sometimes, a sprain will result. There are 3 types of ligament sprains. First-degree sprains are usually overstretched fibers. They heal quickly. A second-degree sprain is a partial tear. Finally, a third-degree sprain is a complete separation from the bone. Surgery will be required at this point.

I lost my balance and fell while spotting a tall client. My sacrum was severely bruised. I also noticed my midback, being extremely tense and inflamed. It was very difficult to work the next day.

I'm an alcoholic and had access to Vicodin because of my history with sports injuries. My injuries include: c7 compression fracture, a broken nose, a complete left ankle fracture, corneal obstruction on my left eye and a hairline fracture on the left hip. Believe me, injuries don't go away. Maintenance is required to stay functional.

After my fall, I could hardly bend forward due to a second-degree sprain of my thoracic and supraspinous ligament. They

limit flexion of the spine. Ligaments connect bones to bones.
They take longer to heal because they have less blood flow.
Fortunately, I was armed with knowledge because of my
experience as a personal trainer and licensed massage
therapist. This included many physical and mental techniques.
"Listen To Your Pain" by Dr. Ben Benjamin and "The Egoscue
Method" by Peter Egoscue, are powerful resources.

The Egoscue method is a series of movements, stretches and
positions. Your body will eventually relearn proper posture
through the repetitive methods. Pain will decrease because of
less compensation.

After a month of the "M*agic 4 L*ower Body Stretches," I was
able to try the Egoscue method. I had no plans of surgery.
Every morning, I tried it at home with my ex-girlfriend. I was
not going to attempt this alone. At the end of the routine, I
would always ask myself a question. Today, what is the level of
pain?

Level one was a great day. Only one Aleve was needed. Level
two was a good day; with just two. Level three required
prescriptions, Flexeril and Vicodin, in the morning and evening.
Level four called for 3 Vicodin, and 3 Flexeril throughout the
day. Level five was an awful day. It took five Vicodin and five

Flexeril; to survive. To further numb the pain; I drank a lot of red wine after work. I drank between 12 to 24 glasses per night. I had at least two, level four or five days every week!

I had two choices. Heal my injury and addiction; or die from an eventual overdose. I was miserable. I had to act strong and amazing for my clients. I was constantly moving with care. One wrong move could mean a muscle spasm. I was always afraid of losing control. Every day was a battle to save my business and life. I was always under the influence of drugs. ABSOLUTELY, NO ONE SHOULD LIVE THIS WAY!

To my understanding, this is a national problem with employment! Americans are failing drug tests because they are testing positive for opiates and other drugs.[1] I don't blame immigrants for coming to the United States. There is so much opportunity here at the home of the drugged and the free! I would come too if I could make money for being sober instead of starving. Thank God, I am self-employed.

Then out of the blue, one of my clients shared an amazing thing with me! He found an alternative way to stop the spread of his terminal illness. I couldn't afford to be complacent. There had

---

[1] Dan Lieberman, "As more Americans fail drug tests, employers turn to refugees," CNN, Last modified, Wednesday March 29, 2017. https://www.cnn.com/2017/03/27/us/refugees-jobs-drug-testing/index.html.

to be other ways to stop pain. So, I began searching.

I started with essential oils. I found ginger and peppermint oil.

Peppermint is a nerve blocker. Ginger soothes tight muscles

and relieves gut discomfort. They gave me temporary

relief. My clients though, started complaining about the aroma

of the combination.

Next, I tried arnica gel. It added 15 more minutes of relief.

Unfortunately, it was in a small tube and very expensive.

Then, I found Calm. It's magnesium citrate. Magnesium is a

natural muscle relaxant. Muscles need calcium to contract and

magnesium to relax. It relaxed my muscles but gave me

horrible diarrhea.

Every week, I was going to a chiropractor and acupuncturist.

They were helping a little, but I was still taking pills and drinking

heavily at night.

While sleeping, you can die from cessation of breathing when

you combine alcohol with opiates.[2] The Centers for Disease

Control and Prevention stated that more than 350,000 people

have died from overdoses involving any opioid. This was

compiled from 1999 to 2016 and included prescription opioids.[3]

---

[2] "What happens when you mix opiates and alcohol," The Recovery
Village, accessed September 30, 2018.
https://www.therecoveryvillage.com/opiate-addiction/faq/mixing-
opiates-alcohol/.

This is highest of all other drug overdoses. Many states are now regulating prescription refill abuse.[4] If one can't get their refill, the next step is heroin. Black Tar heroin laced with other drugs(fentanyl) is easier and cheaper to obtain. Death is the most likely outcome!

One morning, I was looking through the pantry and found various supplements belonging to my ex-girlfriend. I found one with multiple anti-inflammatory benefits.

Inflammation is the process of red, heat, swelling and pain. I took 2 pills with coffee and will never forget the feeling. Within 15 minutes, I felt an amazing pressure release. It was like 20 pounds of air deflated from my body! This was very exciting. Turmeric with its active ingredient curcumin, has always been hailed as a great food supplement. I remember watching Gurmukh Kaur Khalsa stating the importance of turmeric supplementation for health. I researched it.

It can supposedly cause cell apoptosis of certain cancer cells.

---

[3] Seth P. Scholl L, Rudd RA, Bacon S. "Increases and Geographic Variations in Overdose Deaths Involving Opioids, Cocaine, and Psychostimulants with Abuse Potential-United States, 2015-2016." MMWR Morb Mortal Wkly Rep. ePub:29 March 2018.
[4] Michael Laff, "Variety of State Regulations Take Aim at Opioid Abuse," AAFP, Last modified, November 09, 2016. https://www.aafp.org/news/government-medicine/20161109stateconfopioids.html.

It's a blood thinner. It deactivates some virus'. It also detoxes the liver. The main benefit is combating inflammation!

So, I finally had the courage to join Gold's gym after 15 months of just the Egoscue method. I figured if I really hurt myself, someone would call 911 or help me. The purpose of strength training is to prevent injury.

It was still a struggle. There continued to be nights of opiates with alcohol, but I started to see a light at the end of the tunnel...

Two actions changed my life 41 months ago. Daily turmeric with strength training at Gold's gym; and I finally accepted Jesus as my lord and savior.

To truly accept Jesus, you must forgive yourself and forgive all who hurt you. I asked God to please help me recover from pain. He accepted but with conditions. I agreed to LIVE HIS DREAM!

I believe emotions can affect our body. Forgiving and loving others is a good start. Replacing fear with love will raise your life force energy.

Acupuncture opens the *life force* energy pathways of our body. If an energy pathway is blocked, disorder occurs. This creates imbalance, pain and disease.

When I wake up; I drink a large glass of water with apple cider vinegar and lemon. This will acidity your body and enhance calcium absorption. Muscle spasms will decrease as a result.

Then, I get my coffee to relax in my bedroom. On my bed, I have two big pillows set up with my body sized acumat(Kendal Acupressure Massage Mat). The acumat makes sitting sedentary less damaging to your body because it further relaxes the muscles of your back and hip. It also stimulates blood flow and prevents blood stagnation.

Finally, I drink my coffee with 2 pills of turmeric. I read at least 15 minutes of scripture or good works. I am reading the Holy Bible for the 3rd time. I have read the four agreements and Jesus Calling. The good energy of scripture and positive works sets the tone mentally and physically for the rest of the day.

Within 15 minutes, I feel the relief of the curcumin in turmeric. The caffeine in coffee acts as a transporter in the blood. Taking it on an empty stomach accelerates the mode of action. Time to eliminate and shower. Off to work.

When I stand, I practice Chi Gong stance. This allows energy to flow freely throughout the body. This stance also puts the weight of gravity directly on your thighs and abdominal region. This lessens lower back stress. My posture has improved because of this.

I use Doterra Deep Blue and ginger essential oil for minor aches and pains.

In the mid-afternoon, I mix a small cup that includes: two tablespoons of turmeric and ginger spice, one tablespoon of cinnamon and black pepper, a capful of apple cider vinegar and lemon in simmering water. This takes away most of the evening discomforts.

I practice self-care from the Egoscue method and Dr. Ben Benjamin, once or twice a week. Chiropractic and acupuncture are now reserved for emergency situations.

My diet includes a lot of fish, eggs and whole organic foods. I have become a natural competitive bodybuilder with the INBF/WNBF organization since late 2015. I still have left over prescription Vicodin and codeine tablets in my pantry. They are symbolic to defeating my opiate demon.

Today, 09/01/2018, I have been living 1,300 days without taking opiates! The *Seven Lifestyle Changes* are necessary to defeat the opiate demon. HERE THEY ARE...

Lifestyle Change #1

ACCEPTING JESUS with READING GOOD WORKS and SCRIPTURE

Accepting Jesus is what brought everything together. I accepted Jesus as my lord and savior almost 4 years ago.

To do this, you must agree and follow Jesus principles of humility and love. You must forgive yourself and then forgive all who hurt you. This will open your heart and take away all the *pain* from the past. It is amazing how forgiving relieves stress!

Stress contributes to inflammation. Inflammation causes pain and discomfort. Start your day with *the meditation of reading good works.* Read scripture and positive self-help literature such as "The Four Agreements" by Don Miguel Ruiz.

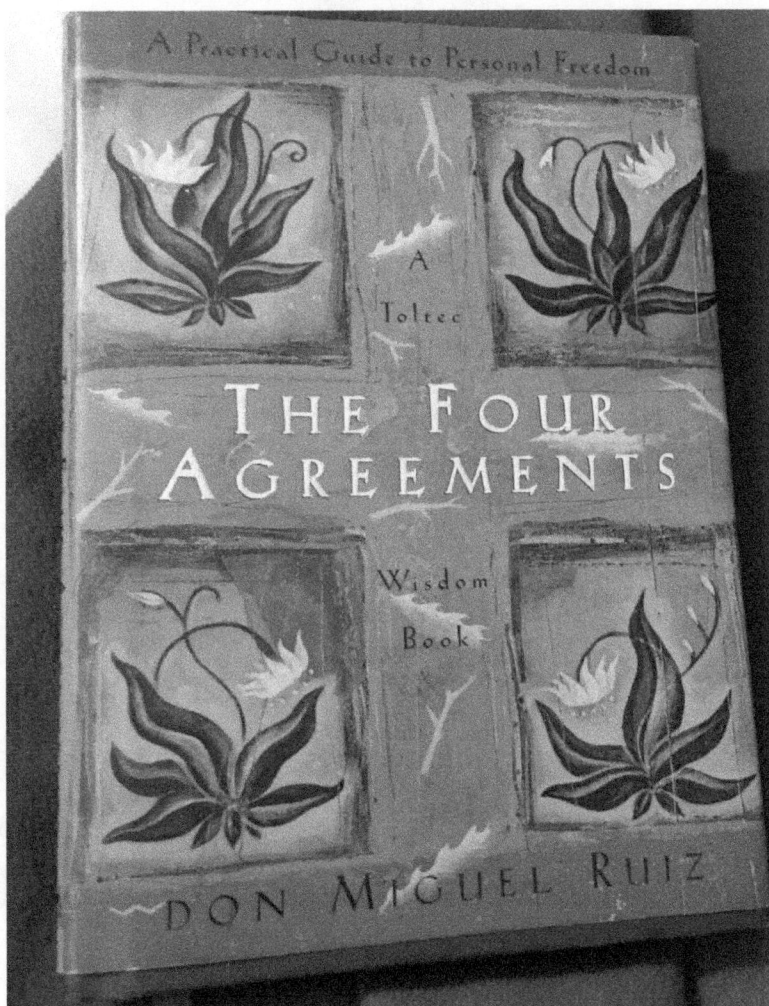

My brain chemistry has changed. Long term clients can tell the difference in my attitude from four years ago. Reading positive works are necessary to heal the mind, body and spirit.

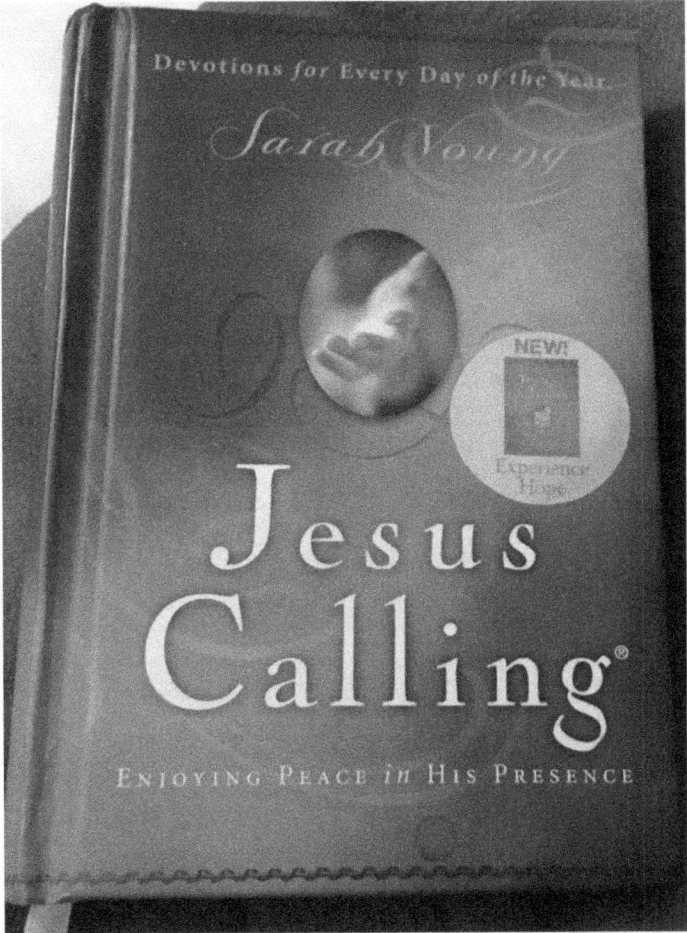

Lifestyle change #2

The MAGIC FOUR LOWER BODY STRETCHES

Self-care is a process that varies individually. If you can stand and walk; *then this could possibly work for you.* I had no plans of surgery. I was determined to beat this injury. At first, I remember the pain and struggle just to be functional. I was always putting up an act at the gym. My business and life were at stake.

The Magic Four Lower Body Stretches helped me to continue working. My very first stretch was the standing hamstring and piriformis stretch. One leg was raised and supported on a bench at a 90-degree angle. The position relieved hip pressure because it was stretching the hamstrings and piriformis. This was the *very* first hint; how the lower body relates to pain. The hamstrings consist of the biceps femoris, semimembranosus and semitendinosus. They work to extend the hip and cause knee flexion. They are in the same region as the sciatic nerve. So, tight hamstrings can cause your hips to tilt anteriorly. The body loves to be in balance. I noticed over time that pain seemed to relieve gradually. I started the stretch at 15 seconds; and eventually held it for 30 seconds up to a minute. Within a few months, I was able to reach more forward with my hand and touch my feet. Eventually, I could reach with my opposite arm to stretch the piriformis, hamstring and back. This is a form of active isolated stretching (AIS) learned from Dr. Ben Benjamin.

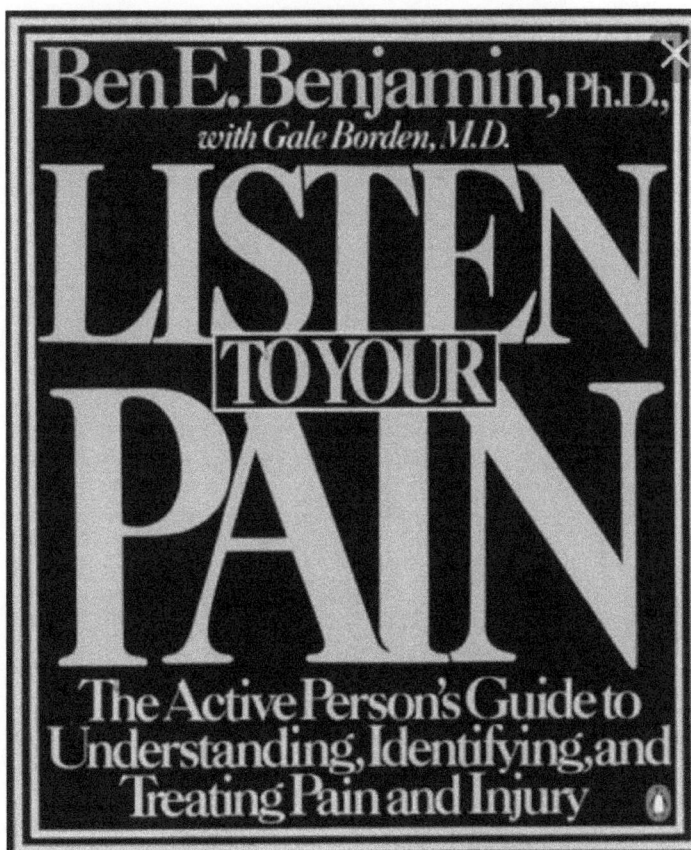

Ben E. Benjamin, Ph.D.,
with Gale Borden, M.D.
LISTEN
TO YOUR
PAIN
The Active Person's Guide to
Understanding, Identifying, and
Treating Pain and Injury

The seated piriformis stretch was next. The piriformis is a short

band of muscle. It originates from your sacrum and then inserts

on the greater trochanter of the femur. It lies on the region of

the sciatic nerve. If it is tight, it will pinch this major nerve.

Symptoms very similar to sciatica will result. This is also known

as Pseudo-Sciatica. This was very hard to do at first because the

back should be straight during the stretch. Over time, the

seated stretch became easier to do. I eventually could straighten my back completely to fully stretch the piriformis.

Then, the quadriceps stretch involved 4 muscles that primarily extend the knee during movement. I was not able to stretch them completely after the fall. This took a month as well. *Keeping the lower body flexible is so important in staying functional.*

Finally, the last of the Magic 4 Lower Body Stretches was the standing foot and calf stretch. The calf muscles are the connection between the foot and the rest of the leg. They help by pulling up the heel during walking or running. After the injury, I noticed that my calves were constantly in a state of contraction. I would stretch them at first by leaning against the wall with one leg extended with heals flat. I eventually placed two dumbbells against a wall and then planted the soles of my feet on the dumbbells. As my flexibility improved, I could bring my hips closer to the wall.

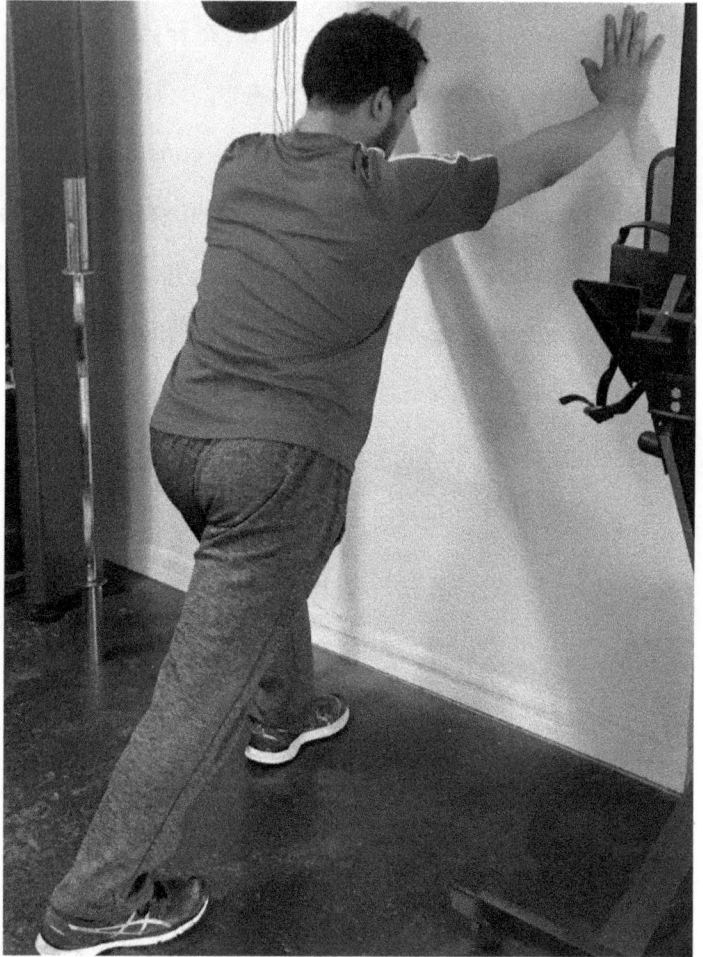

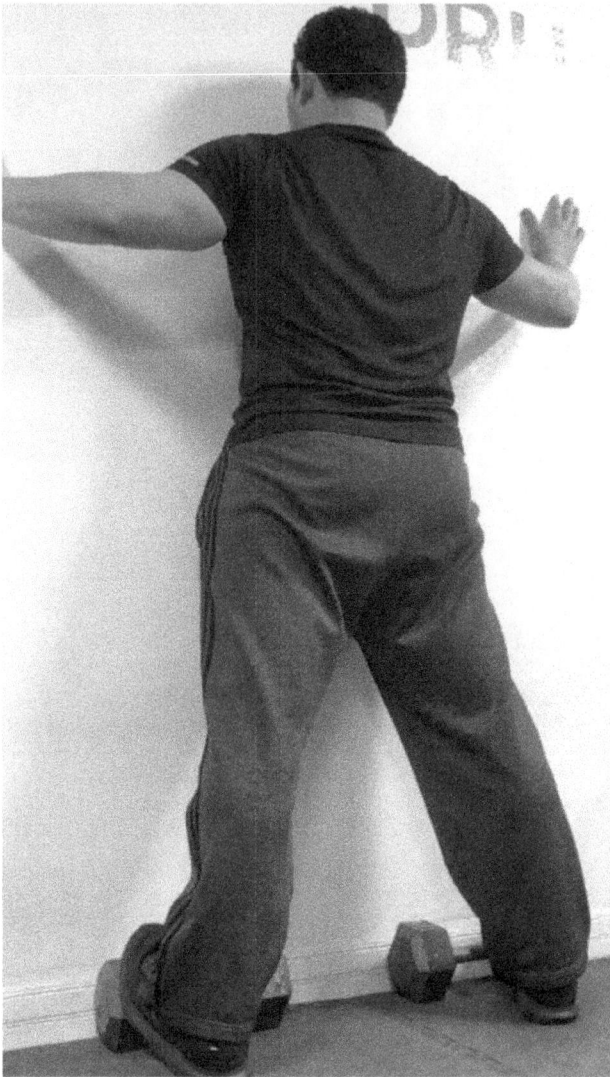

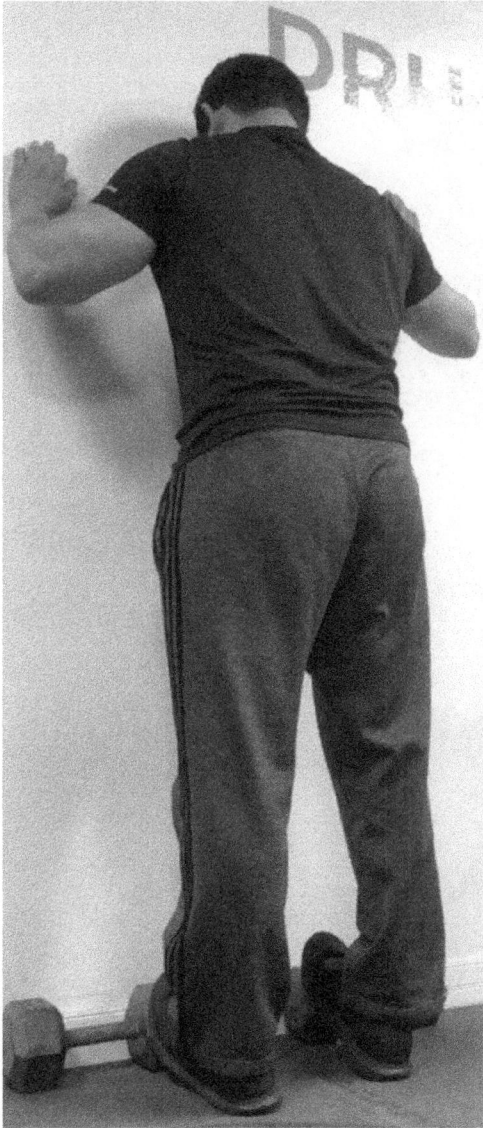

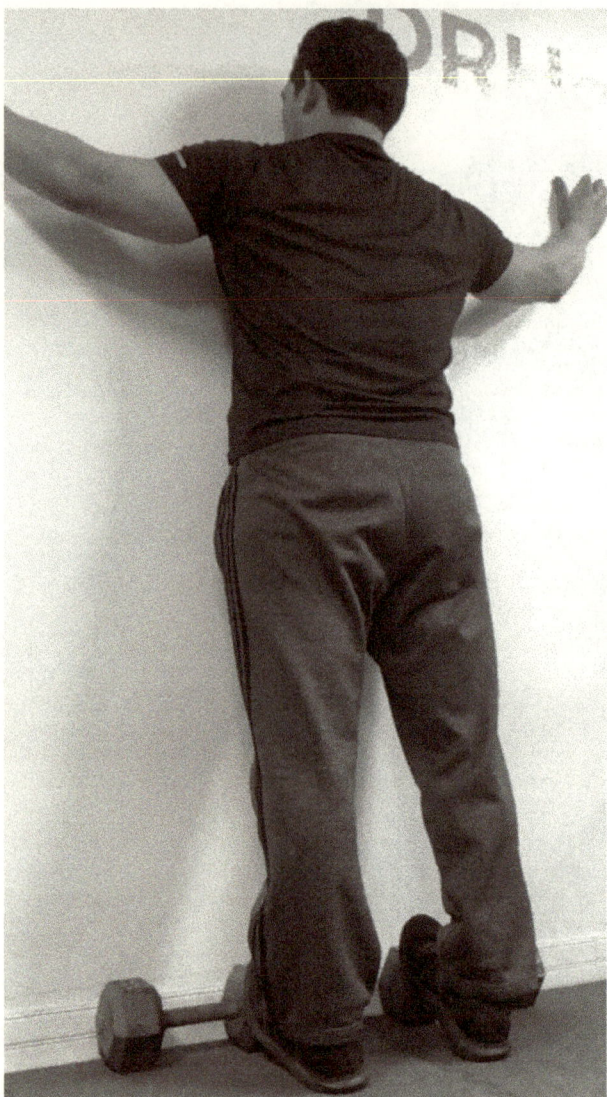

After a month, I was able to try the Egoscue method at home with my ex-girlfriend. The Egoscue method is a series of movements, stretches and positions. They should be easy to do with a balanced posture. Peter Egoscue believed with repetition and time; the body will *balance* and heal itself. The *method prescription* will be based on your posture imbalance. I recommend investigating their website to schedule an appointment.

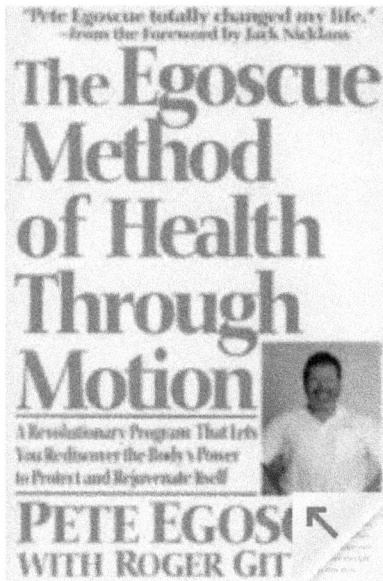

"Pete Egoscue totally changed my life."
—from the Foreword by Jack Nicklaus

The Egoscue Method of Health Through Motion

A Revolutionary Program That Lets You Rediscover the Body's Power to Protect and Rejuvenate Itself

PETE EGOSCUE WITH ROGER GITTINES

Lifestyle Change #3

CHI GONG STANCE

Chi Gong stance is a standing technique that frees the energy pathways of our body. My chiropractor taught me this. When standing with knees bent; it places all the tension on your quadriceps, abdominals and medial sides of the feet. This will strengthen the quads and abdominals. It also relaxes the lower and mid back. Over time, even my posture improved because the leg position does not work well with protracted shoulders. Today, I stand this way. Chi Gong is a non-violent martial art about peace. No wonder, I feel relief with this stance. Peace is one of the highest forms of enlightenment.

Lifestyle Change #4

DAILY TURMERIC with DEEP BLUE and GINGER ESSENTIAL OIL

Turmeric, Doterra Deep Blue and Now ginger essential oil
were all chosen through five years of trial and error. They are
tools to help the day flow with minimal discomfort.

Turmeric is an anti-inflammatory in the skeletal muscle and
tendons. After taking it four years ago, I was able to strengthen
my body. This took several years; but now, I compete as a
natural bodybuilder!

I take two turmeric tablets in the morning with my coffee
on an empty stomach. Some people can't tolerate this; so, take
them with breakfast.

In the mid-afternoon, I mix a small cup that includes: two tablespoons of turmeric and ginger spice, one tablespoon of cinnamon, some black pepper and a capful of apple cider vinegar with a squeeze of lemon in simmering water. This will take away most of the evening discomforts.

Deep Blue and ginger essential oil are amazing tools. Deep Blue
will take away sudden muscular pain. This will be temporary
but very effective.

The ginger relieves pain in the gut and soothes skeletal muscle
aches. If I have an upset stomach, the ginger *usually* relieves
discomfort within 10 minutes!

Lifestyle Change #5

EAT WILD CAUGHT FISH and ORGANIC WHOLE FOODS WHILE DRINKING WATER CONTAINING APPLE CIDER VINEGAR and LEMON

The American diet is so processed and fast. It works with the fast pace of American life. Fast pace equals stress. When you are stressed out; your sympathetic nervous system is activated. You will have vasoconstriction in the gut. Digestion will not be optimal because of the lack of blood flow. Inadequate digestion coupled with the consumption of processed fast food is a recipe for disaster. Stress encourages inflammation. Inflammation contributes to pain. Eating low inflammation foods is a tool to decrease pain. I always feel good after eating wild caught salmon, cod, flounder and tuna. They are a great source of omega 3 fatty acids. Omega 3 fatty acids have been shown to help with depression and arthritis. I feel energetic after eating non-processed whole foods such as kale, carrots, broccoli, spinach and organic eggs. They are nutrient dense. *This is ready energy that the body recognizes.*

I always cook with butter and olive oil.

After my day is finished, I relax and have my meal. This is when the parasympathetic system is optimal. Vasodilation results. Digestion will be optimal because of adequate blood flow. I drink water with two capfuls of apple cider vinegar (ACV) and a few squirts of lemon juice every day. This healed my acid reflux; and prevents muscle cramping.

Eating whole non-processed foods has improved the quality of my life because this will help to decrease *internal* inflammation. The American diet is too processed and unhealthy. This is the cause of obesity in America. Being overweight is uncomfortable and often painful.

Lifestyle Change #6

**USING ACUMATS and
ACUPUNCTURE/MASSAGE/CHIROPRACTOR AS NEEDED**

In this five-year journey, I have discovered some amazing tools.

I found acumats over 3 years ago.

They are amazing body pads with plastic needlelike sticks. They

could pierce the skin. I recommend wearing clothes initially to

protect from being pierced. The needlelike sticks stimulate

blood flow to the areas pressing against it. I have one just for

my back, and another one for the whole backside of my body.

It's amazing how much relief they provide. They prevent blood

stagnation. This is the premise of acupuncture cupping. Blood

stagnation creates discomfort and stiffness in the fascia. Blood

stagnation does not encourage healing. I use my acumats when

I am not working or standing.

Acupuncture is Chinese medicine. Acupuncture has been around for centuries. Acupuncture unblocks the pathways of the body relating to the organs, muscles, bones etc. A blocked pathway creates disorder and imbalance. This will lead to disease or pain. Unblocking these pathways with needles helps to stimulate blood flow and energy to the intended facet of our body. We are energy. Energy that flows freely is better than energy that is blocked. Acupuncture has accelerated the healing process for me. Thank you, Tony Ward, for being a great acupuncturist.

Therapeutic massage is the use of your hands and body to manipulate and soften the fascia. This will encourage fresh blood into the muscle to remove stagnant blood and toxins such as lactic acid crystals etc. I always feel more limber, relaxed and *in less* pain after a good therapeutic massage.

Finding a great chiropractor is important. This is the art of aligning the spine with high velocity adjustments to relieve the pain and discomfort of a subluxated neck or back. I will go to Dr. Burnett at Inner Sun, during emergency situations.

DAILY EXERCISE WITH STRENGTH TRAINING and BODYBUILDING

The worst thing anyone can do is to stop moving. Exercise will keep your mind and body in shape. I started with the Magic Four Lower Body Stretches. This allowed my body to be strong enough for the Egoscue method and exercise. I then strength trained to eventually become a natural bodybuilder.

Natural bodybuilding allows me to take time off from alcoholism. The liver can regenerate itself. This is one of the reasons why I take turmeric. It is a liver detoxifier. Natural competitive bodybuilding gives me a positive outlook on life.

It gives me goals to achieve. Our bodies are temples of God's creation. We must take care of it. Bodybuilding is a way for me to strengthen my whole body.

The strength gains from weight training will help to prevent injuries from reoccurring. My chiropractor, Dr.Burnett, gave me a wonderful tool for pulling. He taught me the *pistol grip.* The pistol grip cancels out the pull of the brachialis muscle. You basically, grip by only emphasizing the baby, ring and middle fingers. You don't use your thumb and index finger. The brachialis muscle is the prime mover in elbow flexion. My back has become so muscular since I started this technique. The added muscle has created more armor and protection. My first pulling movements were *pistol* grip pulldowns to the front and back; followed by rope pullovers with triceps pushdowns. Always start with light weight and complete repetitions in a two to four second tempo. Technique and form are always key. Start with 5 repetitions and increase in 5 repetition increments till you reach 20. Increase resistance by 10 pounds to start the 20-repetition process again. Breathe in through your nose during the eccentric phase; and exhale through your mouth during the concentric phase. *I highly recommend hiring a personal trainer for further instruction.*

I also started strengthening my shoulder and chest with rubber band movements and pushups after weight pulling. These exercises engaged my rotator cuff, chest and rhomboids. The pushups were started from the knees as a precaution. I eventually was able to do full pushups. Upper body stretches were always completed after strength training.

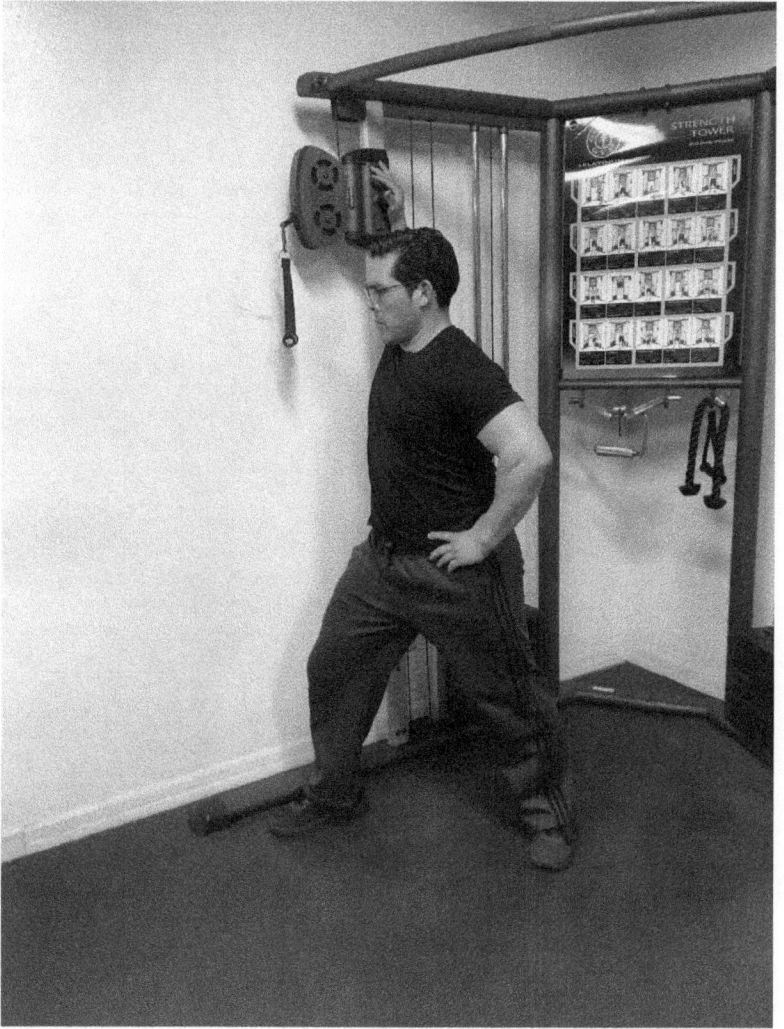

The Chi Gong stance and plank were the first core strengthening

positions. The Chi Gong stance places the weight of

stress on the quadriceps and abdominals while lifting in a

standing position. The plank is basically supporting your

weight with your elbows in a bent arm position and from your

toes with extended legs. You are in prone position. I worked

my way from 10 seconds until I could hold it for 3 minutes.

My first leg strengthening exercises were bodyweight

movements. They consisted of: seated heels to toes, side lying

hip abductions, kneeling hip extensions, standing bodyweight

calf raises and bodyweight squats with an arm counterbalance.

Seated heels to toes, strengthens the muscles on the front of the thigh. They extend the knee, as well as, flex the hip.

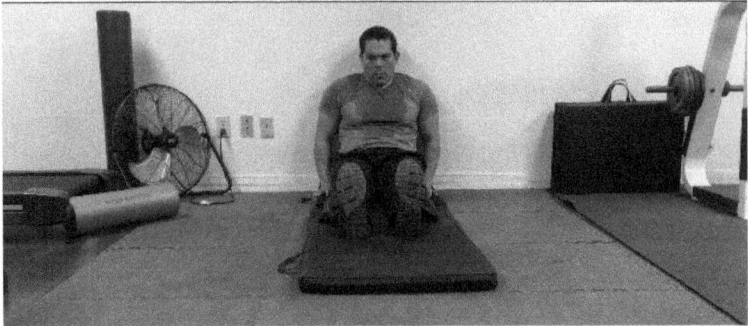

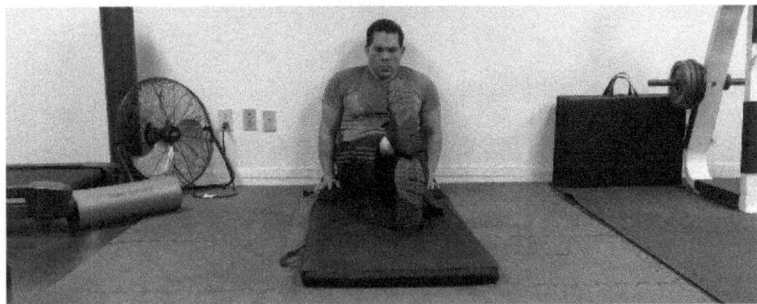

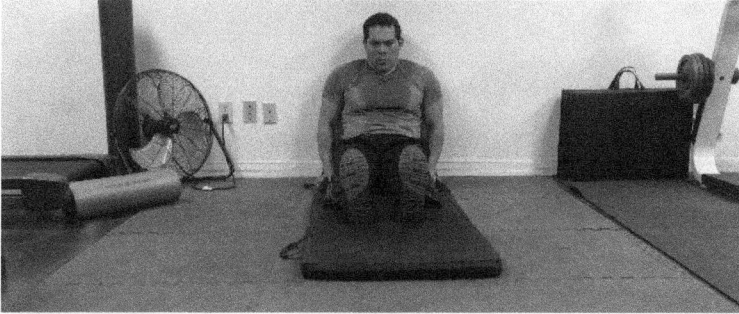

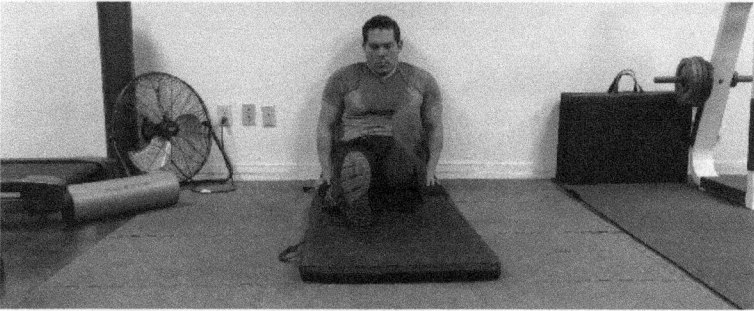

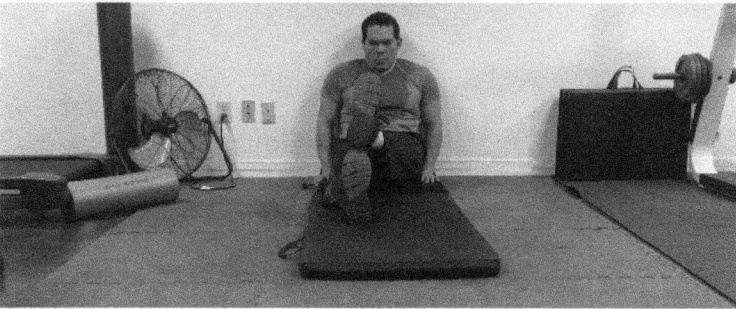

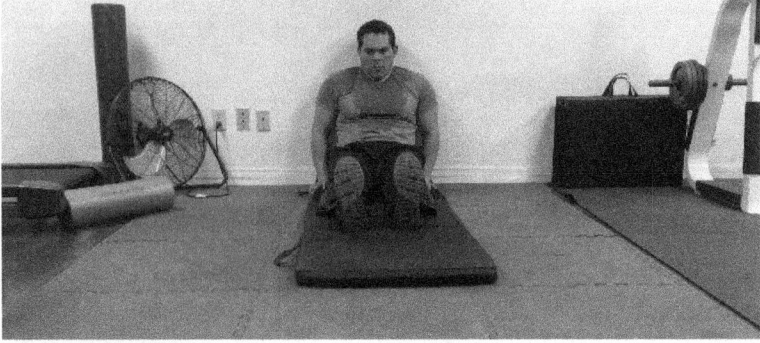

Side lying hip abductions, strengthens the abductors of the hip.

The abductors move the leg laterally.

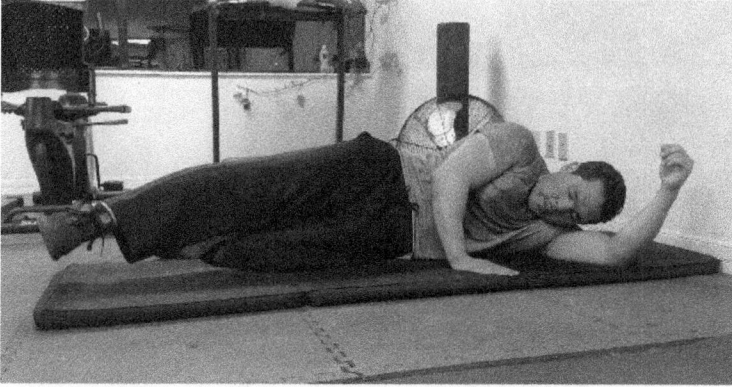

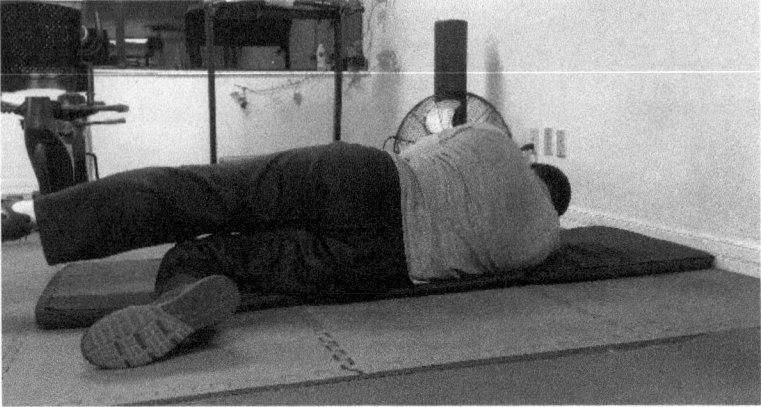

Kneeling hip extensions strengthen the gluteus maximus and minimus, as well as, the hamstrings. These muscles are on the back of the thigh. They extend the hip, as well as, flex the knee.

Standing bodyweight calf raises strengthen the gastrocnemius and soleus, as well as, the muscles below the knee.

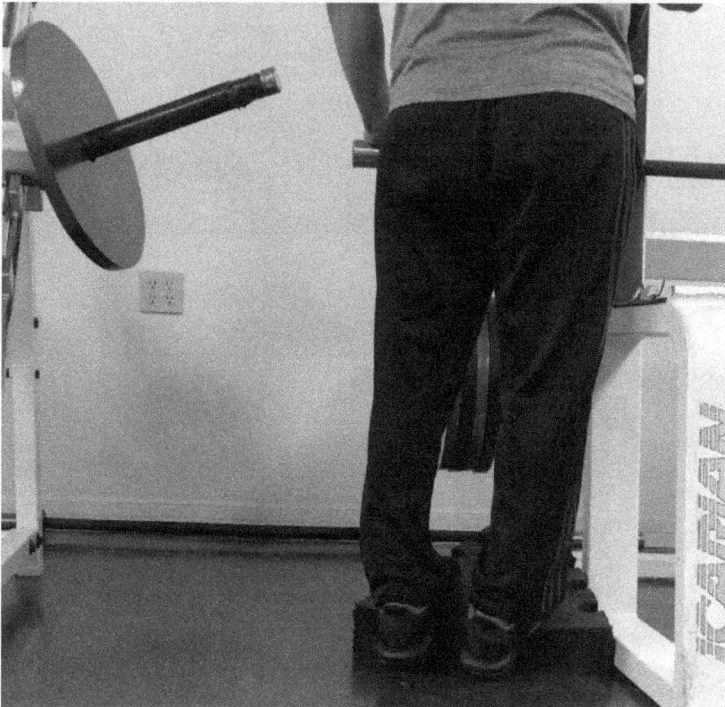

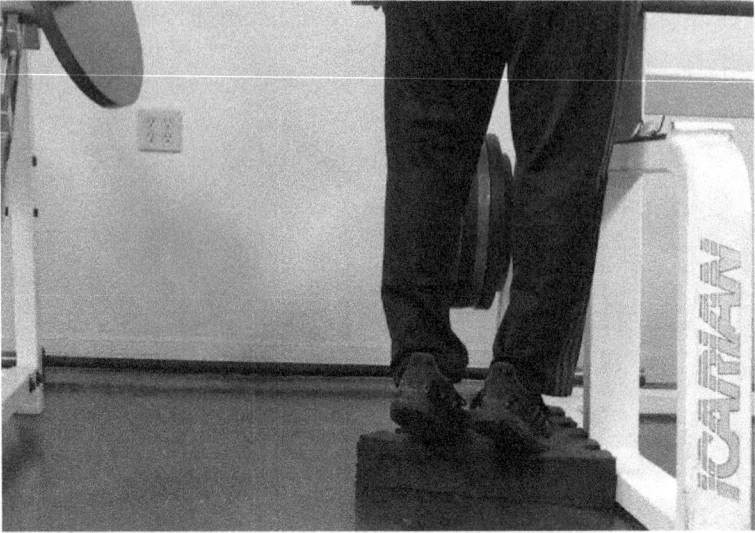
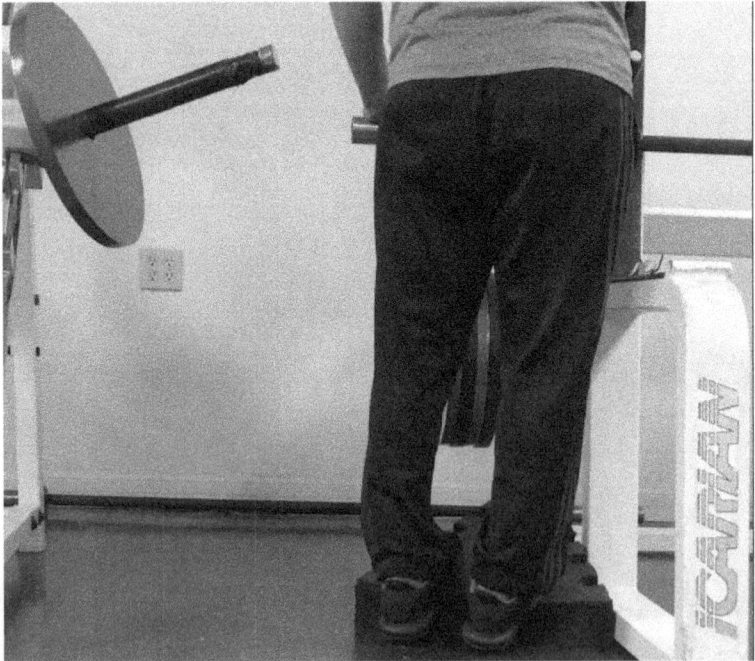

Standing bodyweight squats with an arm counterbalance helped to establish balance and strength throughout my lower body. Feet should be hip width and squeeze your glutes so that your feet will angle correctly. Emphasize engaging your glutes throughout the movement and place your weight on your heels. Raise your arms as you descend and then lower as you ascend.

I eventually graduated to a full bodybuilding routine. This included heavy squats and bench press. This is not within the scope of this message.

CONCLUSION

So, the strengthening process started in 2014. I was struggling but could see the light at the end of the tunnel. I accepted Jesus in 2015. *Everything in life became easier after this.* Healing pain and addiction is a spiritual process. It will require 150% commitment. This entails complete lifestyle changes. It will require faith and asking God(Jesus) for help. You can't go wrong with humility and love. Honoring and caring for your body is loving God. Always listen to what he suggests. This is your instinct.

Today, I can honestly say that I am stronger than the average athlete. At 46 years of age, I am blessed. I will never doubt nor deny Jesus Christ. He made everything possible. The idea of taking opiates no longer fathoms my mind. All I think about now, is how I can bless someone! I am currently training for the 2018 Naturalmania/Pro Universe in White plains, New York. My healing and strength due to the peace of marriage to God(Jesus) has been miraculous. This shows my progress from 2015 till today.

Believe it or not, no doctor or therapist could have done for me what I achieved with God(Jesus). The *Seven Lifestyle Changes were Holy Spirit guided*. They will take care of God's temple, your body. God created us all in his image. We need to honor him through the care and strengthening of the temple. Balance in nature is key.

Full circle, everything in life must be followed with God(Jesus) front and center along with the *Holy Spirit guided, Seven Lifestyle Changes.* This will make DEFEATING THE OPIATE DEMON a definite possibility!

www.ingramcontent.com/pod-product-compliance
Lightning Source LLC
Chambersburg PA
CBHW020955030426
42339CB00005B/109